DATE DUE

NO 1 '04			
JE 7 '06			

DEMCO 38-296

FACING THE RIVER

Facing the River

NEW POEMS BY

Czesław Miłosz

TRANSLATED BY THE AUTHOR

AND ROBERT HASS

THE ECCO PRESS

Copyright © 1995 by Czesław Miłosz Royalties, Inc.

:rved

:ess
l Street
·sey 08525
y in Canada by
Ltd., Ontario
Printed in the United States of America

FIRST EDITION

The text of this book is set in *Sabon*
Designed by Tree Swenson

Grateful acknowledgment is made to the following publications
in which some of these poems first appeared: Antæus: *"This World"*;
Harvard Review: *"To Allen Ginsberg"*; The New Republic: *"Why?,"*
"Sarajevo"; The New Yorker: *"At a Certain Age," "Capri,"*
"Lithuania, After Fifty-Two Years," "The Manor, City of My Youth,"
"Realism," "A Man-Fly," "Woe!," "A Hall," "Body";
Trafika: *"Translating Anna Swir. . ."*

Library of Congress Cataloging-in-Publication Data

Miłosz, Czesław.
Facing the river : new poems / by Czesław Miłosz :
translated by the author and Robert Hass.
p. cm.
1. Miłosz, Czesław—Translations into English. I. Hass, Robert. II. Title.
PG7158.M553A25 1995
891.8′517—dc 20   94-43653
ISBN 0-88001-404-0 (CLOTH)

CONTENTS

FACING THE RIVER

We wanted to confess our sins but there were no takers.
White clouds refused to accept them, and the wind
Was too busy visiting sea after sea.
We did not succeed in interesting the animals.
Dogs, disappointed, expected an order,
A cat, as always immoral, was falling asleep.
A person seemingly very close
Did not care to hear of things long past.
Conversations with friends over vodka or coffee
Ought not be prolonged beyond the first sign of
      boredom.
It would be humiliating to pay by the hour
A man with a diploma, just for listening.
Churches. Perhaps churches. But to confess there what?
That we used to see ourselves as handsome and noble
Yet later in our place an ugly toad
Half-opens its thick eyelid
And one sees clearly: "That's me."

A LECTURE

A certain student in the city of Paris
Coming from countries called Nowhere
Once got a ticket to a lecture
By a famous poet, of the Académie
     Française.

Duchesses and countesses
In gowns of high fashion
In exquisite coiffures
Were honoring the poet.
They, as everyone knew,
Organized for him those evenings
Attended by every person of distinction.

Paul Valéry looked exactly
Like his photographs:
A close-trimmed mustache,
A clear-eyed, attentive
Boy who had gone gray
And was, as always, quick.

He arranged pages on the table.
His hands were precise.
He read logical sequences
Of main and subordinate clauses,
Discussing permanent features
Of aesthetic experience
That confirm the eternal
Attraction of art.

His listener, that student,
Was busy elsewhere:
His hair stood on end,
His ear caught the screams of a hunt,
He was fleeing across frozen fields
Where behind rimed barbed wire
The miserable souls of his friends
And enemies would remain.

Yet he was clever enough
To admire the poet
For his polite acceptance
Of unpleasant circumstances:
These ladies of good will,
The snobs and their approbation,
The cannibalism and wars
Of his century.

For the speaker only pretended
To be among them, with them.
In truth, sitting in his workshop
He was counting verse syllables.
A servant of architecture,
A grower of crystals,
He shunned the unreasonable
Affairs of mortals.

And alas, alas, it passed –
The rejoicing and weeping,
Believing and despairing,
Debasement and terror.
Wind covered the signs with snow,
The earth took in the screams,
No one anymore remembers
How and when it occurred.

And only the sumptuous, golden
Decasyllabic verse
Lasts and will last for its own
Harmonious reason.
And I, late, am returning
With a shred of bitterness
To his cemetery by the sea,
In the always commencing noon.

WHY

Why hasn't it risen, the powerful hymn?
Of thanksgiving, of eternal glory?

Have not the prayers of the humiliated been heard?
The bereft of their possessions, the slandered, the
    murdered, the tortured behind barbed wire?

He broke the teeth from the jaw that devoured the
    humble.
He overthrew the strong one who was to rule for
    centuries.

Monuments of boastful theory lie between nettles.
Darkness descended on the infallible empire.

Is it because generations waited for justice in vain
That faith in superterrestrial verdicts has been
    abandoned?

And the unending valley of faces deprived of hope
Forbids rejoicing to those who are alive.

No *Te Deum* has been sung to praise the Lord of Hosts.
The name of the Hidden God is being pronounced in
    silence.

No painting represents the Warrior in shining armor,
The one who strolls in white clouds over a battlefield.

Who says: "Mine is the punishing arm,
I choose the one day and the one hour in a thousand years."

We were safe behind the shield of his protection.
Misfortunes besieged us but did not prevail.

Where are the solemn assemblies of peoples under a sky
    pierced by the lightning of the One and Holy?
Where is contrite meditation on His deed?

Fearful, they rub their eyes, knowing only that there is no
    limit to evil.
Enough to shout joyfully, and evil will return with force.

They still look for signs in the sky, for fiery circles, rods
    and crosses.
Remembering the word History, the second name of
    which is Annihilation.

CAPRI

I am a child who receives First Communion in Wilno and afterwards drinks cocoa served by zealous Catholic ladies.

I am an old man who remembers that day in June: the ecstasy of the sinless, white tablecloth and the sun on vases filled with peonies.

Qu'as tu fait, qu'as tu fait de ta vie? – voices call, in various languages gathered in your wanderings through two continents. What did you do with your life, what did you do?

Slowly, cautiously, now when destiny is fulfilled I enter the scenes of the bygone time,

Of my century, in which, and not in any other, I was ordered to be born, to work, and to leave a trace.

Those Catholic ladies existed, after all, and if I returned there now, identical but with another consciousness, I would look intensely at their faces, trying to prevent their fading away.

Also, carriages and rumps of horses illuminated by lightning or by the pulsating flow of distant artillery.

Chimneyless huts, smoke billowing on their roofs, and wide sandy roads in pine forests.

Countries and cities that must remain without name, for how can I explain why and how many times they changed their banners and emblems?

Early we receive a call, yet it remains incomprehensible, and only late do we discover how obedient we were.

The river rolls its waters past, as it did long ago, the church of St. Jacob, I am there together with my foolishness, which is shameful, but had I been wiser it would not have helped.

Now I know foolishness is necessary in all our designs, so that they are realized, awkwardly and incompletely.

And this river, together with heaps of garbage on its banks, with the beginning of pollution, flows through my youth, a warning against the longing for ideal places on the earth.

Yet, there, on that river, I experienced full happiness, a ravishment beyond any thought or concern, still lasting in my body.

Just like the happiness by the small river of my childhood, in a park whose oaks and lindens were to be cut down by the will of barbarous conquerors.

I bless you, rivers, I pronounce your names in the way my mother pronounced them, with respect yet tenderly.

Who will dare to say: I was called and that's the reason Might protected me from bullets ripping up the sand close by me, or drawing patterns on the wall above my head.

From a casual arrest just for elucidating the case, which would end with a journey in a freight car to a place from which the living do not return?

From obeying the order to register, when only the disobedient would survive?

Yes, but what about them, has not every one of them prayed to his God, begging: Save me!

And the sun was rising over camps of torture and even now with their eyes I see it rising.

I reach eighty, I fly from San Francisco to Frankfurt and Rome, a passenger who once traveled three days by horse carriage from Szetejnie to Wilno.

I fly Lufthansa, how nice that stewardess is, all of them are so civilized that it would be tactless to remember who they were.

On Capri a rejoicing and banqueting humanity invites me to take part in the festivity of incessant renewal.

Naked arms of women, a hand driving a bow across the strings, among evening gowns, glares and flashes open for me a moment of assent to the frivolity of our species.

They do not need a belief in Heaven and Hell, labyrinths of philosophy, mortification of the flesh by fasting.

And yet they are afraid of a sign that the unavoidable is close: a tumor in the breast, blood in the urine, high blood pressure.

Then they know for certain that all of us are called, and each of us meditates on the extravagance of having a separate fate.

Together with my epoch I go away, prepared for a verdict, that will count me among its phantoms.

If I accomplished anything, it was only when I, a pious boy, chased after the disguises of the lost Reality.

After the real presence of divinity in our flesh and blood which are at the same time bread and wine,

Hearing the immense call of the Particular, despite the earthly law that sentences memory to extinction.

REPORT

O Most High, you willed to create me a poet and now it is time for me to present a report.

My heart is full of gratitude though I got acquainted with the miseries of that profession.

By practicing it, we learn too much about the bizarre nature of man.

Who, every hour, every day and every year is possessed by self-delusion.

A self-delusion when building sandcastles, collecting postage stamps, admiring oneself in a mirror.

Assigning oneself first place in sport, power, love, and the getting of money.

All the while on the very border, on the fragile border beyond which there is a province of mumblings and wails.

For in every one of us a mad rabbit thrashes and a wolf pack howls, so that we are afraid it will be heard by others.

Out of self-delusion comes poetry and poetry confesses to its flaw.

Though only by remembering poems once written is their author able to see the whole shame of it.

And yet he cannot bear another poet nearby, if he suspects him of being better than himself and envies him every scrap of praise.

Ready not only to kill him but smash him and obliterate him from the surface of the earth.

So that he remains alone, magnanimous and kind toward his subjects, who chase after their small self-delusions.

How does it happen then that such low beginnings lead to the splendor of the word?

I gathered books of poets from various countries, now I sit reading them and am astonished.

It is sweet to think that I was a companion in an expedition that never ceases, though centuries pass away.

An expedition not in search of the golden fleece of a perfect form but as necessary as love.

Under the compulsion of the desire for the essence of the oak, of the mountain peak, of the wasp and of the flower of nasturtium.

So that they last, and confirm our hymnic song against death.

And our tender thought about all who lived, strived, and never succeeded in naming.

For to exist on the earth is beyond any power to name.

Fraternally, we help each other, forgetting our grievances, translating each other into other tongues, members, indeed, of a wandering crew.

How then could I not be grateful, if early I was called and the incomprehensible contradiction has not diminished my wonder?

At every sunrise I renounce the doubts of night and greet the new day of a most precious delusion.

A Goddess

Gaia, first-born daughter of Chaos,
Adorned with grasses and trees, gladdens our eyes
So that we can agree when naming what is beautiful
And share with all earthly wanderers our joy.

Let us give thanks in our own and our ancestors' name
For oaks and their rough-barked dignity,
For pines, their trunks flaming in the sun,
For clear green clouds of vernal birch groves
And for the candlesticks of the autumnal wilderness, aspens.

How many kinds of pear and apple trees in our gardens!
(Arranged as described in *The Northern Gardens* of
        Strumillo),
Currants, gooseberries, dogberries, barberries
For a great boiling of preserves
When the faces of our housewives are reddened by their
        long stay by the stove.

There was a separate corner for medicinal herbs,
Those which were grown at the advice of Gizycki's
        Economical-Technological Herbarium.
From them elixirs and ointments for the manor's pharmacy.

And mushroom gathering! Sturdy boletus in the oakwoods.
Strings of them, one by another, drying under the eaves.
A hunter's trumpet is heard when we search for milk cups
And our knives are stained yellow-red by their juices.

Gaia! Whatever happens, preserve at least your seasons.
Emerge from under the snows with the trickling of rivulets
    in springs,
Dress yourself for those who will live after us
If only in the green of mid-city parks
And the blossoming of dwarf apple trees in garden plots at
    the edge of cities.
I depose my petition, your lowly son.

The Manor

There is no house, only the park, though the oldest trees
    have been cut down.
And a thicket overgrows the traces of former alleys.
The granary has been dismantled, white, castlelike,
With cellars where the shelves harbored winter apples.
The same ruts as long ago on the sloping road,
I remembered where to turn but did not recognize the river.
Its color like that of reddish automobile oil,
No rushes and no lily pads.
The linden alley, dear to bees, is gone
And the orchards, a realm of wasps and hornets drunk with
    sweetness,
Disappeared, crumbled into thistles and nettles.
This place and I, though far away,
Simultaneously, year after year, were losing leaves.
Were covered with snow, were waning.
And again we are gathered in our common old age.

My interest turns to the smoke from a metal pipe instead of
    a chimney
Above a cabin haphazardly patched up with boards and
    bricks
In the green of weeds and bushes – I recognize *Sambucus
nigra.*

Blessed be life, for lasting, poorly, anyhow.
They were eating their noodles and potatoes
And at least had the use of all the old gardens
To cut wood for burning in our long winters.

A Certain Neighborhood

I told nobody I was familiar with that neighborhood.
Why should I ? As if a hunter with a spear
Materialized, looking for something he once knew.
After many incarnations we return to the earth,
Uncertain we would recognize its face.
Where there were villages and orchards, now nothing,
    fields.
Instead of old timber, young groves,
The level of the waters is lower, the swamp disappeared
Together with the scent of *ledum*, black grouse, and adders.
A little river should be here. Yes, but hidden in the brush,
Not, as before, amidst meadows. And the two ponds
Must have covered themselves with duckweed
Before they sank into black loam.
The glitter of a small lake, but its shores lack the rushes
Through which we struggled forward, swimming,
To dry ourselves afterwards, I and Miss X, and one towel,
    dancing.

A Naiad

The only proof of the existence of Miss X
Is my writing. As long as I am here
She lives not far from the places she loved.

Her hair was dark blond, nearly chestnut,
Of a tint common among the girls of our gentry.

Her eyes were gray, rarely blue,
More often greenish, the cut of her eyelids
Somewhat oriental. Her cheeks
Would have been protruding if not for her oblong face.
Yet in the arches of her eyebrows something Japanese.

If not for the secret of each singular *anima*
Scoffers would have been right, the trace of a human vanishes.

Yet she is here, in her country
Like an invisible naiad from Mickiewicz's ballad "I Love It."
She will be permitted to go away or rather to fly away
Simultaneously with my disappearance from this world.

Who?

Beyond the red traffic light, young chestnut leaves.
Who is the one who seeing it,
Where does he come from, where will he disappear to,
Who is the one, instead of him,
Who will be seeing the same but not the same thing,
Because of a different pulsation of the blood?

And limbs of huge trees over a steep road,
Leaning into each other, and in that lane,
Beyond the colonnade of trunks, an open brightness.
For whom is this? And how does it vary?
Is it present every time or just imaginary?

Be yourselves, things of this earth, be yourselves!
Don't rely on us, on our breath,
On the fancies of our treacherous and avid eye.
We long for you, for your essence,
For you to last as you are in yourselves:
Pure, not looked at by anybody.

It would be more decorous not to live. To live is not decorous,
Says he who after many years
Returned to the city of his youth. There was no one left
Of those who once walked these streets.
And now they had nothing, except his eyes.
Stumbling, he walked and looked, instead of them,
On the light they had loved, on the lilacs again in bloom.
His legs were, after all, more perfect
Than nonexistent legs. His lungs breathed in air
As is usual with the living. His heart was beating,
Surprising him with its beating, in his body
Their blood flowed, his arteries fed them with oxygen.
He felt, inside, their livers, spleens, intestines.
Masculinity and femininity, elapsed, met in him
And every shame, every grief, every love.
If ever we accede to enlightenment,
He thought, it is in one compassionate moment
When what separated them from me vanishes
And a shower of drops from a bunch of lilacs
Pours on my face, and hers, and his, at the same time.

A MEADOW

It was a riverside meadow, lush, from before the hay harvest,
On an immaculate day in the sun of June.
I searched for it, found it, recognized it.
Grasses and flowers grew there familiar in my childhood.
With half-closed eyelids I absorbed luminescence.
And the scent garnered me, all knowing ceased.
Suddenly I felt I was disappearing and weeping with joy.

TRANSLATING ANNA SWIR ON AN
ISLAND OF THE CARIBBEAN

By banana plants, on a deck chair, by the pool
Where Carol, naked, swims her laps
Of the crawl and the classical style, I interrupt her
Asking for a synonym. And again I am submerged
In the murmuring Polish, in meditation.

Because of the impermanence of the mind and the body,
Because of your tender embracing of our fate,
I call you in and you will be among people,
Though you have written in a poem: "There is no me."
"What a joy there is no me."
Which means neither: "I do not exist,"
Nor: "*Je n'existe pas*," and is pure Slavic:
"*Mene netu*," somewhat Oriental.

And, indeed, by praising being:
    The delight of touch in lovemaking, the delight of
        running on a beach,
    of wandering in the mountains, even of raking hay

You were disappearing, in order to be, unpersonally.

When I saw you for the last time
I understood why they liked neither you
Nor your poetry. With that white mane of yours
You could ride a broom, have a devil for a lover.
And you arrogantly proclaimed
Your philosophy of the big toe,
Of the female split, of the pulse, of the large intestine.

The definition of that poetry: Whatever we do,
Desiring, loving, possessing, suffering,
Is always only meanwhile.
For there must be something else, true and stable.
Though nobody knows what eternity is.

And the body is most mysterious,
For, so mortal, it wants to be pure,
Liberated from the soul which screams: "I!"

A metaphysical poet, Anna Swir
Felt best when she was standing on her head.

TO MY DAIMONION

I

Please, my daimonion, ease off just a bit,
I am still closing accounts and ha.e much to tell.
Your rhythmical whispers intimidate me.
Today for instance, reading about a certain old woman
I saw again—let us call her Priscilla,
Though I am astonished that I can give her any name
And people will not care. So, that Priscilla,
Her gums in poor shape, an old hag,
Is the one to whom I return, in order to throw charms
And grant her eternal youth. I introduce a river,
Green hills, irises wet with rain
And, of course, a conversation. "You know," I say,
"I could never guess what was on your mind
And will never learn. I have a question
That won't be answered." And you, daimonion,
Just at this moment interfere, interrupt us, averse to
Surnames and family names' actualities,
Too prosaic and ridiculous, no doubt.

II

My daimonion, it is certain I could not have lived
     differently.
I would have perished if not for you. Your incantation
Would resound in my ear, fill me,
And I could only repeat it, instead of thinking
About my bad character, the decline of the world,
Or about a lost laundry ticket.
And it seems that while others loved,
Strove, hated, despaired,
I have only been busy with listening intently
To your unclear notes, to change them into words.
I had to accept my fate, called today karma,
For it was as it was, though I did not choose it—
And get up every day to honor the work,
Even if there is no guilt of mine in it and no merit.

III

Two five-year-old boys before the poster of a
    nightclub,
On which a buoyant girl adjusts her garter,
Say something to each other or just stare
At the saurian whiteness of the thigh.

Daimonion, remembering my childhood fears
On this earth of the adults, I grasped who you are.

In their night of distant shooting, fires on the horizon,
Coarse laughter, grapplings, harsh breathing,
The heart of a child is troubled. And you, a wanderer,
Your pity is so strong that you avert your face.

You are a friend of the innocent and the defenseless
Who long for the Kingdom, as was that young rich
    man
So pure that he blushed hearing a lewd word,
And really suffered from it, and probably for that
    reason
After his short life, they raised him on the altars.*

* *St. Stanislaus Kostka*

That was an imprinted effigy of a river:
The flow of a knotty main branch, twigs of affluents,
As if they wanted to merge,
Trees and swift water, the best things on earth.
The façade, inlaid with marble panels,
Towered over a plain of rotting streets,
Some of them, without end, stretched beyond the
       horizon,
Where, in the smoke of garbage cans, in leprous
       desolation,
The poor squat, intent on killing each other,
And, arms ready, police cars make rounds.
When the bus took us to a ritual at the museum,
We heard beyond the windows yells, jeering,
Then we were met by smiles and silence.

So much guilt behind them and such beauty!
These landscapes, in the quiet splendor
Of early summer, toward evening, these coves
Of lakes amid lush green, when, for welcome,
Messengers come running, in saffron robes,
And bring gifts, huge balls made of light.
Or his portraits. Is not tenderness
Needed to drive a brush with such attention
Along the eyelids of a sorrowing eye
Through the furrow at lips closed by grief?
And how could he do it? Knowing what we know
About his life, every day aware
Of harm he did to others. I think he was aware.
Just not concerned, he promised his soul to Hell,
Provided that his work remained clear and pure.

If not for the existence of Earth, would there be a
    Hell?
The instruments of torture are man-made:
Kitchen knives, choppers, drills, enemas.
And implements to create the hellish noise:
Trombones, drums, a mechanical flute, a harp
With a poor damned man entwined in its strings.
The waters in Hell are set by the cold of eternal
    winter.
Mass meetings, military parades on ice
Under the blood-red and smoke-dark glow of burning
    cities.
Fire blazing from windows—not sparks, human
    figures,
Small and black, fly out and then fall into a chasm.
Dirty taverns with wobbly tables. Women in kerchiefs
Cheap, you can have them for a pound of meat,
And a multitude of busy henchmen,
Deft, well trained in their trade.
Thus it's possible to conjecture that mankind exists
To provision and to populate Hell,
The name of which is duration. As to the rest,
Heavens, abysses, orbiting worlds, they just flicker a
    moment.
Time in Hell does not want to stop. It's fear and
    boredom together
(Which, after all, happens). And we, frivolous,
Always in pursuit and always with hope,
Fleeting, just like our dances and dresses,
Let us beg to be spared from entering
A permanent condition.

REALISM

We are not so badly off, if we can
Admire Dutch painting. For that means
We shrug off what we have been told
For a hundred, two hundred years. Though we lost
Much of our previous confidence. Now we agree
That those trees outside the window, which probably
    exist,
Only pretend to greenness and treeness
And that the language loses when it tries to cope
With clusters of molecules. And yet, this here:
A jar, a tin plate, a half-peeled lemon,
Walnuts, a loaf of bread, last—and so strongly
It is hard not to believe in their lastingness.
And thus abstract art is brought to shame,
Even if we do not deserve any other.
Therefore I enter those landscapes
Under a cloudy sky from which a ray
Shoots out, and in the middle of dark plains
A spot of brightness glows. Or the shore
With huts, boats, and on yellowish ice
Tiny figures skating. All this
Is here eternally, just because once it was.
Splendor (certainly incomprehensible)
Touches a cracked wall, a refuse heap,
The floor of an inn, jerkins of the rustics,
A broom, and two fish bleeding on a board.
Rejoice! Give thanks! I raised my voice
To join them in their choral singing,
Amid their ruffles, collets, and silk skirts,
One of them already, who vanished long ago.
And our song soared up like smoke from a censer.

Did I fulfill what I had to, here, on earth?
I was a guest in a house under white clouds
Where rivers flow and grasses renew themselves.
So what if I were called, if I was hardly aware.
The next time early I would search for wisdom.
I would not pretend I could be just like others:
Only evil and suffering come from that.
Renouncing, I would choose the fate of obedience.
I would supress my wolf's eye and greedy throat.
A resident of some cloister floating in the air
With a view on the cities glowing below,
Or onto a stream, a bridge and old cedars,
I would give myself to one task only
Which then, however, could not be accomplished.

WOE!

It is true, our tribe is similar to the bees.
It gathers honey of wisdom, carries it, stores it in
     honeycombs.
I am able to roam for hours
Through the labyrinth of the main library, floor
     to floor.
But yesterday, looking for the words of masters
     and prophets
I wandered into high regions
That are visited by practically no one.
I would open a book and could decipher nothing
For letters faded and disappeared from the pages.
Woe! I exclaimed—so it comes to this?
Where are you, venerable one, with your beards
     and wigs,
Your nights spent by a candle, griefs of your wives?
So a message saving the world is silenced forever?

At your home it was the day of making preserves.
And your dog, sleeping by the fire, would wake up,
Yawn and look at you—as if knowing.

The wrought iron of the gate at Pierson College
And my stint there, which resembles
Nothing in my past life. Forgetting
And remembering. Both, how strange.
That old professor with an accent,
Who gives a seminar on *The Possessed* and reads
In the Beinecke Library manuscripts:
Joseph Conrad's *Heart of Darkness*
Hurriedly written with a pencil, a neat
Script of the novel *Razumov*
Called later *Under Western Eyes.*
Is he identical with a boy
Who, starting from Bouffalowa Hill
Would walk Louis home along Mala Pohulanka
And then goes to Tomasz Zan Library
To get a book of sea adventures?
On the very edge. Just before falling:
Now, here. Before "I" changes into "he."

Quality passes into quantity at the century's end
For worse or better, who knows, just different.
Though for those students no Louis ever
Existed and the old professor's passionate tone
Is a bit ridiculous as if the fate of the world depended
                    on truth.

SARAJEVO

—Perhaps this is not a poem but at least I say what I feel

Now that a revolution really is needed, those who once were fervent are quite cool.

While a country murdered and raped calls for help from the Europe which it had trusted, they yawn.

While statesmen choose villainy and no voice is raised to call it by name.

The rebellion of the young who called for a new earth was a sham, and that generation has written the verdict on itself,

Listening with indifference to the cries of those who perish because they are after all just barbarians killing each other

And the lives of the well-fed are worth more than the lives of the starving.

It is revealed now that their Europe since the beginning has been a deception, for its faith and its foundation is nothingness.

And nothingness, as the prophets keep saying, brings forth only nothingness, and they will be led once again like cattle to slaughter.

Let them tremble and at the last moment comprehend that the

word Sarajevo will from now on mean the destruction of their sons and the debasement of their daughters.

They prepare it by repeating: "We at least are safe," unaware that what will strike them ripens in themselves.

Allen, you good man, great poet of the murderous century, who persisting in folly attained wisdom.

I confess to you, my life was not as I would have liked it to be.

And now, when it has passed, is lying like a discarded tire by the road.

It was no different from the life of millions against which you rebelled in the name of poetry and of an omnipresent God.

It was submitted to customs in full awareness that they are absurd, to the necessity of getting up in the morning and going to work.

With unfulfilled desires, even with the unfulfilled desire to scream and beat one's head against the wall, repeating to myself the command "It is forbidden."

It is forbidden to indulge yourself, to allow yourself idleness, it is forbidden to think of your past, to look for the help of a psychiatrist or a clinic.

Forbidden from a sense of duty but also because of the fear of unleashing forces that would reveal one to be a clown.

And I lived in the America of Moloch, short-haired, clean-shaven, tying neckties and drinking bourbon before the TV set every evening.

Diabolic dwarfs of temptations somersaulted in me, I was aware of their presence and I shrugged: It will pass together with life.

Dread was lurking close, I had to pretend it was never there and that I was united with others in a blessed normalcy.

Such schooling in vision is also, after all, possible, without drugs, without the cut-off ear of Van Gogh, without the brotherhood of the best minds behind the bars of psychiatric wards.

I was an instrument, I listened, snatching voices out of a babbling chorus, translating them into sentences with commas and periods.

As if the poverty of my fate were necessary so that the flora of my memory could luxuriate, a home for the breath and for the presence of bygone people.

I envy your courage of absolute defiance, words inflamed, the fierce maledictions of a prophet.

The demure smiles of ironists are preserved in the museums, not as everlasting art, just as a memento of unbelief.

While your blasphemous howl still resounds in a neon desert where the human tribe wanders, sentenced to unreality.

Walt Whitman listens and says, "Yes, that's the way to talk, in order to conduct men and women to where everything is fulfillment. Where they would live in a transubstantiated moment."

And your journalistic clichés, your beard and beads and your dress of a rebel of another epoch are forgiven.

As we do not look for what is perfect, we look for what remains of incessant striving.

Keeping in mind how much is owed to luck, to a coincidence of words and things, to a morning with white clouds, which later seems inevitable.

I do not ask from you a monumental *oeuvre* that would rise like a medieval cathedral over a French flatland.

I myself had such a hope, yet half-knowing already that the unusual changes into the common.

That in the planetary mixture of languages and religions we are no more remembered than the inventors of the spinning wheel or of the transistor.

Accept this tribute from me, who was so different, yet in the same unnamed service.

For lack of a better term letting it pass as the practice of composing verses.

A HUMAN FLY

Crowds, streetcars stopped—is it a demonstration?
In the city of Oakland, in the year 1919?
All of them, obviously, in hats, looking up.
No, not at a speaker. It is a human fly
Who climbs vertically the wall of a building.

O miserable human fly, arms spread aloft,
You move inch by inch, testing a handhold.
And below, those hats. Will he fall? Or make it?

They stand in the photograph, lovers of plebeian
     games,
Of matches in a ring, acrobatics under the tent of a
     wandering circus,
Of catch-as-catch-can, of blood in the arena.
I am not a lover of mankind, though I pretended,
As if my tender skin, my fastidiousness were not
     against.

—But these here, hot-blooded, how many eyes,
Muscles, varieties of chin, shapes of lips,
All must be dead.
They are shadows, no more.

—And it is just that such a short existence had been
     their store.

HOUSE IN KRASNOGRUDA

I

The woods reached water and there was immense silence.
A crested grebe popped up on the surface of the lake,
In deep water, very still, a flock of teals.
That's what was seen by a man on the shore
Who decided to build his house here
And to cut down the primeval oak forest.
He was thinking of timber he would float down the Niemen
And of thalers he would count by candlelight.

II

The ash trees in the park calmed down after the storm.
The young lady runs down a path to the lake.
She pulls her dress over her head
(She does not wear panties though Mademoiselle gets angry),
And there is a delight in the water's soft touch
When she swims, dog-style, self-taught,
Toward brightness, beyond the shade of the trees.

III

The company settles into a boat, ladies and gentlemen
In swimming suits. Just as they will be remembered
By a frail boy whose lifeline is short.
In the evening he learns to dance the tango. Mrs. Irena
Leads him, with that smirk of a mature woman
Who initiates a young male.
Out the door to the veranda owls are hooting.

Her polka-dot dress—that's all I know of her.
Once, walking silently with my gun in a forest
    thicket
I stumbled upon her lying with Michael
On a blanket spread in the clearing.
A plump little thing,
They say she was an officer's wife.
Her name must have been Zosia.

To the black waters I arrived at dusk.
All of them are dead, it was long ago.

Peace to you, Zosia, and to your adventures.

Going on a vacation, is it not usual
To expect that something might happen:
A dark-haired man from the cards, or a blond one
    like Michael,
Just for some change in everyday yawning,
Calls to a girlfriend, cake in a tea shop.
We are induced to sin by boredom and curiosity,
But besides that we are innocent.

You should understand, Zosia, what trouble I have
When I want to think of your life attentively
And find here, where you are mine, what is unique
In you, though it's covered by common form.

Perhaps you helped build a barricade.
Perhaps you sacrificed yourself for a sick child.
Perhaps, suffering pain from a wound or illness,

You came to a high degree of resignation.
However it was, whether you perished with your
    burning city,
Or, old, wandered in it, not recognizing the streets,
I try to be everywhere with you, yet in vain.
And all I can do is touch your too-round breasts
Remembering your dress, red, with white polka-dots.

PLATO'S DIALOGUES

Always at the end of the week my father and I would go to the sauna on Tartar Street.

There was a solemnity in our being allotted narrow sofas in a common hall with compartments like those in a railway wagon.

And in our opening the door into everything different, dense steam darkening the light of the bulbs and making the naked figures hardly visible.

From a faucet one would fill a wooden bucket with cold water for dousing one's head, and carry it to the highest shelf, as high as one could bear, among the roars of naked males lashing themselves with birch rods.

Virile ambition required one to stay there till the skin, made oversensitive by heat, would feel every touch of the rod as a whiplash.

Emitting roars belonged to the rite and testified that one was reaching the limit of endurance.

Upon our return to the hall we would listen to conversations conducted by fat men, everyone on his sofa, wrapped in his sheet:

Permanent customers, well-to-do artisans, police officers, and Jewish merchants.

Their conversations would not deserve the name of Plato's dialogues, but almost.

On the Banks of the Niemen was published in 1888. This bucolic Polish novel is the work of Eliza Orzeszkowa, one of the "emancipated" women of that time. Although Orzeszkowa received only the superficial education proper to young ladies of the manor, political events catapulted her into an independent literary career. Because of a Polish uprising against Russia in 1863, her husband was deported to Siberia. The marriage—unsuccessful from the start—disintegrated, but divorce proceedings dragged on for years. Her farm was confiscated, and she herself, considered a dangerous democrat by the tzarist authorities, was placed under police surveillance; for most of her life she was forced to live in the provincial town of Grodno (in what is now Belarus). She turned to writing to sustain herself. A virtual prisoner, she acquired (through extensive reading in several languages) a wide education, and her stories and novels defended the cause of the underprivileged, that is, women and Jews. Her characters were drawn from the people she observed in her province—peasants, Jewish artisans, and the petty gentry.

On the Banks of the Niemen takes place in a village and its neighboring manor. In the manor lives a young woman named Justine, a poor cousin of the owner. Instead of looking to a marriage that would free her from her lowly position, she falls in love with Jan, a lad of the village, and marries him, thus affirming her readiness to labor with her hands and assume the status of a peasant. The novel is full of political allusions, somewhat toned down because of censorship. A few miles from the village, in the forest, is the mass grave of the insurrectionists of 1863, where many boys from the village are buried. Jan and Justine's visits to the grave strengthen the bond between them through the awareness of a common cause. They also pay visits to the preserved tomb of the founders of the village, Jan and Cecilia. According to legend, a girl of royal blood, a long, long time ago, eloped with a commoner, and the couple came to live in the primeval forest, gradually clearing it and settling with their progeny; all the inhabitants of the village bear the same name, Bohatyrowicz, and boast a coat of arms given to them by a king who, while hunting, stumbled by chance upon a flourishing settlement in the depths of the forest. These two graves carry the novel's message about the value of tradition, of an uninterrupted continuity, passed from generation to generation, of attachment to ancestral land.

The candles burned out long ago, Justine.
Other people walk your paths by the Niemen.
While I enter into a union with you, quite amorous.
I touch the heavy black tresses
That you, just now, are loosening. I weigh in my palm
Your no doubt abundant breast. I look in the mirror
At your gray eyes and the deep red of your lips.
You are big, strong, broad-shouldered.
Twenty-four, you don't like to be called
Young lady. And your dreams are telling.
No reason to be ashamed in front of me, who comes
    from an epoch
That will be called shameless. Mrs. Orzeszkowa
Would stop her pen. Your romance with your cousin
Left to our guesses, the flow of blood,
Spots on the linen, passed over in silence.
Yet for me your fleshliness, Justine,
Is important, you have to appear entire
So that your pride and angry integrity
Shine, surprising. Where do they come from?
What dialogues go on between the body and soul?
In your land, good and evil were measured by the
    grave.
Who would remain faithful to it, who would not.
(In other words, a serious corrective
Was introduced into the tangle of motives and desires.)
That novel can't be summarized for foreign readers.

In you they would find only another woman
Proclaiming equality of classes, like George Sand.
And now, Justine, comes old age, a ready chapter.
But not to be written by Mrs. Eliza.
You gave birth to sons and daughters, grandchildren
    grew up.
You rest your hands on a gnarly cane, the mother of a
    tribe,
The last of your kin and your contemporaries.
In floury snow you see sledges, convoys of sledges.
You hear the shouts of soldiers, women's laments.
And you know, feel, that this is how it looks, the end
Of one earthly country. Never again an echo
Of a song sung on the Niemen, the flight of swallows.
Never again fruit harvests in the village orchards.
The bars of cattle cars slam, one after another.
They carry you, by ancient trails, to a land of shadows
    and murders.
Though you never existed, let us light candles,
Here, in our study, or in our church.

And wax encrusts sconces and nations trade and whales dance near Lahaina and the ungrateful generations raise their buildings and French policemen get new capes and the sun rises once again and . . .

I always think of Orzeszkowa with love and respect. She is for me an example of a writer who served the good. She certainly knew much about the dark side of human existence, but she preferred, for reasons she considered superior, not to divulge that knowledge. Just as she rarely let show her erudition. She described the small people of her province with the sympathy of a person who appreciates simple, traditional virtues.

A strange adventure befell me. I was reading—I don't know which time—*On the Banks of the Niemen* and I found myself falling in love with Justine. When she looked in the mirror, I was by her side, and it seemed to me that she could see my voyeur's eyes. I was thinking about her, and out of that thinking came a poem, "Undressing Justine." The novel, set in the nineteenth century, was not enough for me; my imagination suggested a later fate for the heroine. After all, the inhabitants of the village of Bohatyrowicze had before them World War I and the independent Poland of the interwar years, but also the abyss that opened in 1939 with the entrance of the Soviets. For me this was not history learned from textbooks; it's a thing torturing me still with tears of compassion. I counted years. In 1939, Justine would have been a very old woman, but her arrest and deportation to the East is by no means beyond the limits of probability, since some million and a half people were uprooted in that way.

I concede that I did not know that Orzeszkowa had not invented the village of Bohatyrowicze, or the legend of its founding, including the tomb of the first settlers Jan and Cecilia. Or that the tale of Justine, a girl from the manor, and Jan, a country lad, was based on a true story. All this I learned from an article that recounted a visit to present-day Bohatyrowicze. Moreover, I learned that my anxiety about Justine's fate was justified and my poem was just short of prophetic.

The reporter had heard the story from the mouth of an elder of the tribe, Stanislaw Bohatyrowicz, who lives in one of the few surviving houses in the village. Everything was as it was in Orzeszkowa, even the tomb of Jan and Cecilia, dated 1547, and the grave of the insurrectionists in the forest. "We used to go there often by the river. Now I am old and do not go there anymore, but I know from people that Father Lucian Radomski from Lunna (that is our parish) has cleaned up the grave with his parishoners, and that it's a nice place now. So there are traces of our remembering them, those who were buried there in 1863. They were many, and our boys from Bohatyrowicze also lie there. The manor in reality bore the name of Miniewicze. All that remains of it are ruins." Is that the same place that belongs to the Korczynskis in the novel? "Yes, Mrs. Orzeszkowa only changed the names. All the rest is the same. That daughter of Kamienski in the novel, she was nearly a spinster. She fell in love with a boy from the village, and he with her. In the novel they are Jan and Justine. But, to be exact, he wasn't a Bohatyrowicz. He descended from us on his mother's side, and she married a certain Strzalkowski. So, you see, Mrs. Orzeszkowa changed the name. That 'Jan,' I remember, was a handsome boy, and he married the lady Kamienska from the manor. Later old Kamienski died, and 'Jan' became the owner of the estate. They had two children, a daughter and a son. Sophie entered a monastery. Perhaps she's still alive. She used to visit us, even after the war. And the son, Casimir, stayed here; he managed the estate, and before that he studied in Warsaw where he met his wife.

"Jan and Justine did not live in the manor, but very near. Jan built a house for them between the village and the manor. It's still standing, but it's quite dilapidated. And in 1939 when the Soviet troops came and our Poland was perishing, all the landowners in the neighborhood, including Casimir and his old father, were taken and executed, near here, in a village called Kwasowka. Then when the Germans invaded our region, Mrs. Justine exhumed their remains secretly and buried them in the cemetery at Lunna."

So, perhaps some peculiar currents circulate between a literary work, its readers, and the posthumous life of its characters. It was so long ago. The novel appeared in 1888. Such cataclysms rolled over the earth, and yet the reality of that time persists in gossip, in an orally transmitted tale, in correctives to the myth. Justine was not, in reality, a poor relation, but a daughter of the manor's owner, Kamienski, Korczynski in the novel, who had served many years in Siberia.

Mrs. Orzeszkowa is still spoken of in the village as an acquaintance. A woman of the younger Bohatyrowicz generation tells the reporter that the novelist found her grandfather a wife in a neighboring village. "So that beautiful Mary Obuchowicz in the novel, she's my grandmother. She married Adam, my grandfather. When a son was born to them, Mrs. Orzeszkowa and her husband Nahorski were the godparents. They helped with his education. Later he perished in Katyn."

Probably a commentary is impossible, as, until now, no language has been invented comprehensible to both the living and the dead.

RETIRED

An old man, tapping with his cane, aware of his silence.

Which fills every corner of his body with a dense, burning lava.

And confirms the trustworthiness of the words of Jesus about a worm that does not die and fire that never goes out.

Surrounded by his children and grandchildren, he sits down in a wicker armchair on the porch of his house.

Voices of birds from the garden are for everyone, he muses, they do not care about me, neither do they know.

And I, instead of screaming and beating my head against the floor, admire the cloudless sky.

Soon that tale, never started, will pass away and I with it.

A cat sleeps in the sun, the world continues and does not need the signs of testimony.

For nothing would have resulted from them, except the realization that we are poor humans.

Guardians of prison trains, then prisoners ourselves, the torturers and the tortured.

Only I do not understand why I should constantly remember those things.

And accuse myself of events stronger than myself.

Longing for the thunderbolt of a stroke to liberate me from images of this earth.

An old man, serene, liked by his neighbors—he greets passersby, and envies them their innocence.

That is what they have, he muses, if they have not been submitted to a test.

WANDA

Wanda Telakowska (1905–1985), once a popular figure in artistic Warsaw, a painter specializing in color woodcuts, was renowned for her conspicuous stature, her organizing skills, and her sense of humor. In the interwar period she created pattern designs for the textile industry based on folk craft, in particular the handwoven fabrics of Eastern Poland. Her idea of beauty in things for everyday use stemmed in part from native sources (the theories of the poet Norwid), and in part from folk art. She received some backing for her project in government circles. Also a cooperative—called *Lad,* or *Harmony*—working along those lines, was founded in Warsaw.

The *oeuvre* of Telakowska, the colored woodcuts and the theoretical essays prepared by her for print, was consumed by fire during the Warsaw Uprising of 1944. After the war she saw the possibility of organizing state enterprises to produce, for internal use and for export, products of high artistic quality modeled on native handicraft. She met with resistance, and the transition from prototypes to mass production proved impossible. A collection of individual objects, sent to New York, was much admired by the big trading firms, which, however, wanted quantity. Telakowska traveled to America in 1948, hoping to secure markets for the export of textiles. She succeeded in interesting prospective buyers, but no supply from Poland was forthcoming. I tried to help her. Unfortunately, her case—of a socially minded person eager to serve her country—was typical of Poland at that time.

And so, Wanda of a bygone Warsaw,
Let the living pretend they are not concerned
With death, which is too common, too ordinary.
But I don't understand how it is possible

To live and to know that the hour strikes,
And to wait quietly for one's turn.
Something needs to be done. Protest marches?
Wallowings, howlings, curses?
At least let there be a skeleton with a scythe,
Scissors of the Fates, or a star that plummets
When a soul departs. But there is nothing,
An obituary in two or three lines,
And then oblivion forever.

We did not become romantically involved.
Traveling, we would take two rooms.
Because sex is diabolic. I believed that then
And still maintain it. And whoever
Believes otherwise surrenders to the power
Of the Spirit of the Earth, who is not good.

We are allowed it, but only with our spouses.
And, besides, Wanda, you were not a temptation.
Huge, heavy, and not too pretty,
A good companion in coarse laughter at the
        table.
And beneath, another Wanda, timid and
        tenderhearted,
Mindful—though with shame—of her maidenhood.

In our sorrows we find solace in a project:
To make the State a helper of art.
Factories and mills were to create beauty
For everyday, as country looms once did.

The elegant wives of ministers listened.

(Oh, elegant wives of ministers!
Where are you? In what department of oblivion
Do you touch up your lips, snap your handbags?)

During the war I used to meet Wanda at the Iwaszkiewiczes in Stawisko. From her accounts of wartime adventures I remember those testifying to her presence of mind—for instance, when she found herself in the middle of a roundup at the edge of Mokotowski Field, by Polna Street. "They were taking everybody, they walked straight toward me. What could I do? At the last moment I squatted and lifted my skirt. The German gendarme felt, after all, awkward confronted with a woman pissing and passed by, pretending he did not see me." Or when she moved to the mountains after the Warsaw Uprising and lived in Zakopane with a peasant family. "They were banging on the door. I escaped to the yard. There was a shed with sheep. I had brought my fur-lined overcoat from Warsaw, so I turned it fur-side-up and got down on all fours among the sheep. The Germans took a look into the shed and went away."

———————

To be a witness, try to remember.
That cannot be done. Nor am I doing it.
I only know it's gone, that city,
And on its ruins the illustrious Red Army.
Also Wanda, who tried to convince yokels
Who pick their noses behind their desks
That it's worthwhile, important, that the State
    should . . .

Dull and sluggish, without the gentry or the Jews,
They were doing something, not too much.
And all daring seemed to them lordly,
Too risky, fanciful.

While you, Wanda, were of those who were
    ready
To straighten the bent axis of the globe.
People, as usual, did not care.
And soon, old age. Perhaps, you kept in memory
That trip of ours to San Francisco,

Which we both had hope enough to undertake.
What use medals and crosses of merit?
You remained alone in your defeat,
Lonely, not needed, going blind.

To bear it. And human beings bear it.
And what can be said is always too late.

TO MRS. PROFESSOR IN DEFENSE OF
MY CAT'S HONOR AND NOT ONLY

My valiant helper, a small-sized tiger
Sleeps sweetly on my desk, by the computer,
Unaware that you insult his tribe.

Cats play with a mouse or with a half-dead mole.
You are wrong, though: it's not out of cruelty.
They simply like a thing that moves.

For, after all, we know that only consciousness
Can for a moment move into the Other,
Empathize with the pain and panic of a mouse.

And such as cats are, all of Nature is.
Indifferent, alas, to the good and the evil.
Quite a problem for us, I am afraid.

Natural history has its museums,
But why should our children learn about
    monsters,
An earth of snakes and reptiles for millions of
    years?

Nature devouring, nature devoured,
Butchery day and night smoking with blood.
And who created it? Was it the good Lord?

Yes, undoubtedly, they are innocent,
Spiders, mantises, sharks, pythons.
We are the only ones who say: cruelty.

Our consciousness and our conscience
Alone in the pale anthill of galaxies
Put their hope in a humane God.

Who cannot but feel and think,
Who is kindred to us by his warmth and
        movement,
For we are, as he told us, similar to Him.

Yet if it is so, then He takes pity
On every mauled mouse, every wounded bird.
Then the universe for him is like a Crucifixion.

Such is the outcome of your attack on the cat:
A theological, Augustinian grimace,
Which makes difficult our walking on this earth.

You whose name is aggressor and devourer.
Putrid and sultry, in fermentation.
You mash into pulp sages and prophets,
Criminals and heroes, indifferently.
My *vocativus* is useless.
You do not hear me, though I address you,
Yet I want to speak, for I am against you.
So what if you gulp me, I am not yours.
You overcome me with exhaustion and fever.
You blur my thought, which protests,
You roll over me, dull unconscious power.
The one who will overcome you is swift, armed:
Mind, spirit, maker, renewer.
He jousts with you in depths and on high,
Equestrian, winged, lofty, silver-scaled.
I have served him in the investiture of forms.
It's not my concern what he will do with me.

A retinue advances in the sunlight by the lakes.
From white villages Easter bells resound.

It appears that it was all a misunderstanding.
What was only a trial run was taken seriously.
The rivers will return to their beginnings.
The wind will cease in its turning about.
Trees instead of budding will tend to their roots.
Old men will chase a ball, a glance in the mirror—
They are children again.
The dead will wake up, not comprehending.
Till everything that happened has unhappened.
What a relief! Breathe freely, you who suffered much.

HAPPENINGS ELSEWHERE

"I can't possibly go to Hell, me, so nice and good,"
Exclaimed Adam, boy, when the devils clustered around him.
They were dressed in black and had red snouts.
They taunted him horribly, pricking his sides with pitchforks
(They used small ones for emergency purposes.)

"I did not believe devils exist,"
Moaned poor Adam, boy,
"I have met ones like you are but that was on the earth."

"He-he"—they answered—"nonexistence is our specialty.
And you, do you exist, you scrap? You existed an instant
        and basta.
Now you will take your seat with us in nothingness forever."

"What did I do"—lamented Adam, boy,
"What did I do, that you have me in your power?"

"You don't know? He-he, don't worry, you'll get the idea.
We have everything recorded, documented."

They were walking along a slope where they had
        caught him in his lonely march
By lying in ambush in an empty cabin, as frontier guards are wont
        to do,
In that no-man's-land, not far from the gates of Hell.

Mountains, bare, sulfur-colored, in the semidarkness
Descended toward a dim and uncertain plain.
They were leading him down, now he was silent.

Then a shot resounded, so loud it was probably earthly.
The echo rolled and hardly had it thundered away
When the devils began to shrink as if punctured and leaking air.
Then they disappeared completely and again he was alone.

Then one in a homespun jerkin, in long boots,
Swinging a shotgun from his shoulder, came close and stood
       above him.

—"You did a lot of mischief, Adam boy, you are
       always in trouble.
Where did you get the idea that you are innocent?
Did you really believe you could sin without guilt?
I am sent to announce the verdict.

"You'll be with the Hospitaliers. There, festering bedsores,
Vapors of decaying flesh, howlings,
And pain, crying for vengeance to Heaven,
Contradict continuously the goodness of God.
In other words, the cruel cosmic vaudeville goes on.
It's different from Hell, instead of nothingness
Uninterrupted duration and suffering.

Once it was called Purgatory. And there you will serve,
Washing, lifting, cleaning up, listening.
And every day you will learn to know your guilt,
Until you concede that you deserve no better."

Then a messenger went ahead up the steepness,
Adam, boy, followed him, for, alone, he could not find the way.

A HALL

The road led straight to the temple.
Notre Dame, though not gothic at all.
The huge doors were closed. I chose one on the side,
Not to the main building—to its left wing,
The one in green copper, worn into gaps below.
I pushed. Then it was revealed:
An astonishingly large hall, in warm light.
Great statues of sitting women—goddesses,
In draped robes, marked it with a rhythm.
Color embraced me like the interior of a purple
        brown flower
Of unheard-of size. I walked, liberated
From worries, pangs of conscience and fears.
I knew I was there as one day I would be.
I woke up, serene, thinking that this dream
Answers my question, often asked:
How is it when one passes the last threshold.

AFTER ENDURING

The hypothesis of resurrection
Drawn by an eminent scientist from quantum
    mechanics,
Foresees our return to familiar places and people
After a billion or two billion earth years
(Which in the beyond-time equals one instant.)
I am glad I have lived long enough to witness the
    fulfillment of predictions
About a possible alliance of religion and science,
That was prepared by Einstein, Planck, and Bohr.
I do not take too seriously scientific phantasies,
Though I respect graphs and computations.
The same was expressed more concisely by Peter the
    Apostle,
When he said: *Apokatastasis panton,*
The renewal of all things.
Yet it is helpful: to be able to imagine
That every person has a code instead of life
In an eternal storage room, a supercomputer of the
    universe.
We disintegrate into rot, dust, microfertilizers,
But that code or essence remains
And waits, till at last it takes flesh.
And also, as the new corporeality
Should be cleansed of evil and afflictions,
The notion of Purgatory enters the equation.
Not different is what the faithful in a country church
Repeat in chorus asking for life eternal.
And I with them. Not comprehending
Who I will be when I wake after enduring.

BODY

The human condition is not pain only.
Yet pain rules us and has much power.
Wise thoughts fail in its presence.
Starry skies go out.

From the center of the anatomical atlas
Where liver-red and clear-red of lungs
Meet flesh-color of cloudlike intestines,
Heralds of pain proceed with their muted calls.
From defenseless guard posts at the frontier of the skin
Runs the alarm of being touched by steel or fire.

No chitinous or horn armor.
Nakedness under dresses and the masks of dancers.
And our obsession with undressing them on the stage
To know what they are when they pretend.

Scarlet liquor under the sun of the heart
Circulates, warms up, pulsates.
Visions, landscapes move to its rhythm
As does the brain, a gray moon, Luna.

On a gynecological chair open knees.
Defenseless viscera shattered by childbirth.
And the first scream, terror of exile into the world,
On a frozen river, in a stony city.

Julia, Isabel, Luke, Titus!
It's us, our kinship and mutual pity.
This body so fragile and woundable,
Which will remain when words abandon us.

You were my beginning and again I am with you, here, where I
learned the four quarters of the globe.

Below, behind the trees, the River's quarter; to the back, behind
the buildings, the quarter of the Forest; to the right, the quarter of
the Holy Ford; to the left, the quarter of the Smithy and the Ferry.

Wherever I wandered, through whatever continents, my face was
always turned to the River.

Feeling in my mouth the taste and the scent of the rosewhite flesh
of calamus.

Hearing old pagan songs of harvesters returning from the fields,
while the sun on quiet evenings was dying out behind the hills.

In the greenery gone wild I could still locate the place of an arbor
where you forced me to draw my first awkward letters.

And I would try to escape to my hideouts, for I was certain that I
would never learn how to write.

I did not expect, either, to learn that though bones fall into dust,
and dozens of years pass, there is still the same presence.

That we could, as we do, live in the realm of eternal mirrors,
working our way at the same time through unmowed grasses.

II

You held the reins and we were riding, you and me, in a one-
horse britzka, for a visit to the big village by the forest.

The branches of its apple trees and pear trees were bowed down
under the weight of fruits, ornate carved porches stood out above
little gardens of mallow and rue.

Your former pupils, now farmers, entertained us with talks of
crops, women showed their looms and deliberated with you
about the colors of the warp and the woof.

On the table slices of ham and sausage, a honeycomb in a clay
bowl, and I was drinking *kvas* from a tin cup.

I asked the director of the collective farm to show me that village;
he took me to fields empty up to the edge of the forest, stopping
the car before a huge boulder.

"Here was the village Peiksva" he said, not without triumph in
his voice, as is usual with those on the winning side.

I noticed that one part of the boulder was hacked away,
somebody had tried to smash the stone with a hammer, so that
not even that trace might remain.

III

I ran out in a summer dawn into the voices of the birds, and I
returned, but between the two moments I created my work.

Even though it was so difficult to pull up the stick of *n*, so it
joined the stick of *u* or to dare building a bridge between *r* and *z*.

I kept a reedlike penholder and dipped its nib in the ink, a wandering scribe, with an ink pot at his belt.

Now I think one's work stands in the stead of happiness and becomes twisted by horror and pity.

Yet the spirit of this place must be contained in my work, just as it is contained in you who were led by it since childhood.

Garlands of oak leaves, the ave-bell calling for the May service, I wanted to be good and not to walk among the sinners.

But now when I try to remember how it was, there is only a pit, and it's so dark, I cannot understand a thing.

All we know is that sin exists and punishment exists, whatever philosophers would like us to believe.

If only my work were of use to people and of more weight than is my evil.

You alone, wise and just, would know how to calm me, explaining that I did as much as I could.

That the gate of the Black Garden closes, peace, peace, what is finished is finished.